LIST BROWSE FOR SALESFORCE

IMPLEMENTATION GUIDE

TO A FINISH SALESFORCE APPS
BOOK 1

JOSEPH DINDINGER

WISE PATH BOOKS

List Browse for Salesforce, Implementation Guide

ISBN: 978-1-959666-05-9

Published by:

Wise Path Books

a division of To A Finish LLC

12407 N MoPac Expy #250

Austin, TX 78758

www.wisepathbooks.com

CONTENTS

INTRODUCTION

LIST BROWSE INTRODUCTION AND PHILOSOPHY

This chapter introduces the user to Salesforce.com, the To A Finish organization and the List Browse app

This brief manual is an introduction to List Browse and the philosophy behind this popular app. For those eager to get going, the first chapter can be skipped in favor of a quick implementation of the List Browse App.

ICON KEY

- Details You Can Skip
- Don't Miss This!
- Sample Code
- Danger!

To succeed in configuring and installing List Browse you will need to pay close attention to all of the information contained in this manual, especially Chapter 2.

The Icon Key to the left shows the icons you will be seeing as you go through this manual. The more advanced readers can skip some of the details as indicated by the appropriate icon.

This manual is a work in progress, so please do take notes and let us know if you run into any issues with the text or if you believe there is a better way to accomplish the tasks we describe.

INTRODUCING SALESFORCE.COM

Salesforce.com's CRM solution is broken down into several broad categories: Sales Cloud, Service Cloud, Data Cloud (including Jigsaw), Collaboration Cloud (including Chatter) and Custom Cloud (including Force.com). Below, we'll highlight a few of them.

The Sales Cloud

The Sales Cloud includes a real-time sales

collaborative tool called Chatter, provides sales representatives with a customer profile and account history, allows the user to manage marketing campaign spending and performance across a variety of channels from a single application, tracks opportunity-related data including milestones, decision makers, customer communications, and other information unique to the company's sales process. Automatic email reminders can be scheduled to keep teams up to date.

Other activities on the Salesforce cloud include using the Jigsaw business data to access business contacts, and designing and automating processes in Salesforce CRM.

The Service Cloud

The Service Cloud provides companies with a call center-like view that enables them to create and track cases coming in, and automatically route and escalate what's important. The Salesforce CRM-powered customer portal provides customers the ability to track their own cases, includes a social networking plug-in that enables the user to join the conversation about their company on social networking websites, provides analytical tools and other services including email, chat, Google search, and access to customers' entitlement and contracts.

The Force.com Platform

Salesforce.com's platform as a service (PaaS) product is known as Force.com. The Force.com platform allows external developers to create add-on applications that integrate into the main salesforce.com application and are hosted on Salesforce.com's infrastructure.

These applications are built using Apex (a proprietary Java-like programming language for Force.com) and Visualforce (an XML-like syntax for building user interfaces in HTML or Flex).

You can continue reading more on Salesforce.com at WikiPedia.com.

INTRODUCING TO A FINISH

To A Finish™ is a concept company that has grown out of a desire to improve the Salesforce CRM consulting industry. Too often we have found the priorities of consulting companies skewed towards speed and profitability, rather than excellence and long-term success. This is not a blanket statement about all consulting companies, rather a general statement of the industry at large.

We believe there is a different way of consulting that will bring ultimate success to any CRM venture. The biggest difference is time. We give special attention to steps that are often rushed or even overlooked entirely in a typical project. Things like in-depth analysis, getting to really know a business, documentation and end-user involvement in the process help us set up a project for success. Ultimately, we must spend the time to do the work until it is absolutely complete; To A Finish™.

We are not guaranteeing our clients will never see a bug or have to rethink initial strategies. Reworking is actually part of the process of achieving success. What we are saying is that our strategies and focus will minimize unforeseen problems and achieve for us an ultimately successful project completion. We put our name on our work and stake our reputation on quality service.

Test us. Allow us to show you the difference of doing work To A Finish™.

You can find more about To A Finish at www.toafinish.com

When you finish a thing you ought to be able to say to yourself: "There, I am willing to stand for that piece of work. It is not pretty well done; it is done as well as I can do it; done to a complete finish. I will stand for that. I am willing to be judged by it."

- O.S. Marden

INTRODUCING LIST BROWSE

The philosophy behind the List Browse app is the ability to quickly browse data without requiring multiple screen changes.

With standard Salesforce.com configuration, in order to view two records on a list view, you must first click one record, and when finished go back in your browser and then click the other record. This is fine for two or three records, but when reviewing multiple records, it can get confusing and time consuming.

We have two different browse experiences for Classic, which are covered in a different document, and only one in Lightning:

Paid Objects
Free Objects
Lightning
All Objects *
Contact, Account
Classic
*All Objects **
Contact, Account
Legacy Classic
*All Objects ***
*Five Standard Objects ***

** Does not include some non-standard objects like Notes and Events.*

*** In Legacy Classic mode, most objects are available, but due to clickjacking protection,* *legacy mode is often unavailable, and if available, often read only, depending on settings.*

List Browse allows you to first **select the records** you want to browse, and click "Browse" to go to the first record.

Note that if you put it at the end of the Search Layout, it might be hidden in the "More" buttons.

Then, simply browse the selected records by moving forward (or back) through the list.

A list of what each navigational element does is below. We trust that you will find these are simple controls that will give you back time in your day.

List Browse Control Guide

These are the simple controls you will learn to use and hopefully love.

Control

Description

This control, and its contrary twin, will take you one record either before or after the current one on the list. If it is grayed out, that means you are on the first or last record.

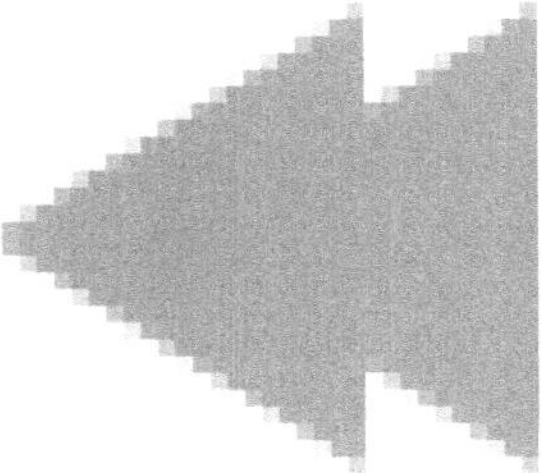

This control, and its opposite, takes you to the first or last record on your list. If it is grayed out, it means you are already there.

This button will show you a list of any Browse Lists that you have previously saved in the current object. By clicking on the name of the list, you will switch to that list as the active Browse List (and lose the current active Browse List).

This button will allow you to save the current active Browse List with a name of your choice in order to pull it up later.

This button will show you a list of all the records in the current Browse List. It allows you to skip ahead or behind to any particular record by clicking on it.

This button will clear the current active Browse List and take you out of List Browse for the current object until you again click the Browse button, OR it will simply close the browse element until you have clicked Browse again, depending on what you have configured in the Configuration page.

BEFORE YOU BEGIN, REQUIREMENTS

Before you begin working with List Browse, you must have several components already in place and configured. We will not cover these components in detail, but will at least point you to where you can get the information you need.

Licensing

A production and/or sandbox system Salesforce.com Org will be needed in order to set up the integration. The following types of licenses are all supported:

- Sales Cloud
- Service Cloud
- Custom Cloud (Force.com)

Editions

At the current time, only the following editions will support List Browse. The Group edition is not supported.

- Enterprise
- Unlimited and Up
- Developer
- Professional* (most functionality)

Lightning and My Domain

Please note that this app will absolutely need the My Domain feature to be turned on and activated for all users in order to use the standard version of List Browse. The reason for these requirements is that a Lightning Component is being installed as a part of the upgraded package.

For more information on the My Domain feature, see the Salesforce documentation:

https://help.salesforce.com/articleView?id=domain_name_overview.htm

Once you deploy "My Domain", you cannot change it without contacting Salesforce support, so please be careful.

CHAPTER 1

INSTALLING AND CONFIGURING LIST BROWSE

In this chapter you will learn how to quickly install the app and then configure it for use in standard and custom objects

SEVERAL BASIC STEPS must be completed in order to install and configure List Browse in your Salesforce.com org, no matter which version you use. Any user with administrative skills should be able to install and configure the app.

The main steps necessary to complete are listed below.

Step

Description

1 Install the List Browse app

2 Add the Browse button to the objects you want to browse

3 Create custom Browse buttons for any custom objects or other standard objects where it is needed

4 Add the Browse component to the Lightning Page

5 Leave **List Browse** a 5-Star Review on the AppExchange!

INSTALLING THE LIST BROWSE APP

The first step is to install the app from the AppExchange. You should be able to find the app easily by searching for "List Browse" on the AppExchange.com website.

Click on the **Get it Now** button on the listing and log in to the AppExchange using your Salesforce.com credentials (if you are not already).

Next, you will need to decide the type of Org you want to install the app into. You can try List Browse in a sandbox first, but generally speaking you should be able to install it into a Production system with no adverse effects.

After selecting one, click the **I have read and agree to the terms and conditions** (you might want to look at those first) checkbox and then press the **Confirm and Install!** button.

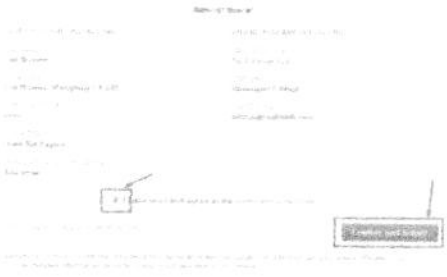

You will be asked to log in. Do so, and the installation will continue in your Org. After logging into the org you want to install into, go through the install process. The only important choice will be who to install for. Select **Install for all users** and press the **Install** button.

CONFIGURING THE LIST BROWSE APP

Before you can use List Browse, you must simply add the **Browse** buttons to the six standard objects that are supported by default. The six objects that come standard are:

- Leads

- Accounts
- Contacts
- Opportunities
- Cases
- Tasks

Note

For most versions of Salesforce, you can create a Browse button for other standard or custom objects as well as the standard ones. Doing that is covered in the next section.

In order to add the Browse button, you must first go to the **Setup** section, by clicking the Gear Icon (shown to the right) in Lightning, or clicking your name at the top of the page and selecting Setup.

Permission Set Setup

In order to have access to List Browse, users

will need to be granted the List Browse User permission set. In the Setup area go to Users Permission Sets and then click on the **List Browse** permission set. (You will also need to do this for regular users with the **List Browse (NonAdmin)** permission set.)

Now, click the "Manage Assignments" button and add all the users who will be accessing List Browse to this permission set, including System Administrators.

Now, you are ready to proceed.

Configuring the Browse Buttons

Once in the Setup section, click on the **Object Manager** tab and then search for the object you want to browse, this example uses the Account object (the free version only works with Accounts and Contacts). Click on it and then on the **Search Layouts for Salesforce Classic** menu option. (Yes, even if in Lightning!) **Edit** the "List View" item:

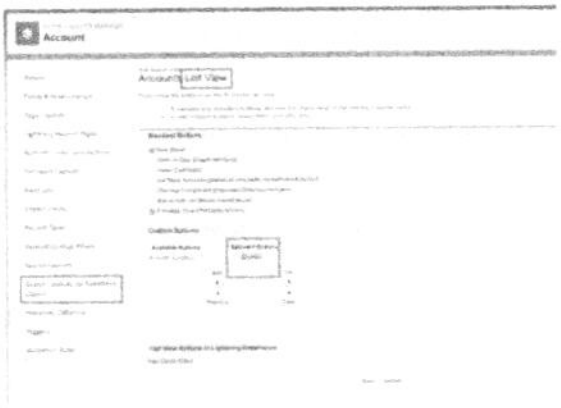

Save this page and back out of Setup. **Click on the tab** for the object you are setting up, in this example, Accounts. Now go to a list.

Once you select records and press the Browse button, you are taken to the first record. Click the Gear Icon once again and this time select **Edit Page**. This will take you to the Lightning App Builder. From the "Custom – Managed" section on the left panel, drag the ListBrowse Component somewhere on the page.

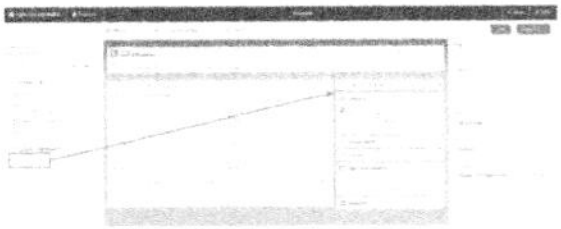

Now, **Save** and if necessary, release the page to be the Org Default, or to as many profiles as you would like. When done, click the Back button and begin browsing your records.

You are now finished adding the Browse button to all the Leads list views. You may now repeat the process for the Accounts, Contacts, Opportunities and Cases in order to add the Browse button to those objects as well. If you selected the "Browse (Legacy)" button, that is all you need. If you are using the newer "Browse" button, keep reading.

If you want to expand List Browse to use it in objects outside of Opportunities, Accounts, Contacts and Leads, please follow the instructions in the next chapter.

KNOWN ISSUES

At this point in our development cycle, List Browse is very stable. However, a list of known issues will be kept on this page:

1. Certain lists will break the "Browse" button. These lists have non-standard features which break the underlying Salesforce commands that our application uses in order to detect which records have been selected. We hope that the bug will be fixed in a future Salesforce version, but until

then, you might run into an error similar to this one when you try to Browse:

core.apexpages.exceptions.ApexPagesHandledException: Object type not accessible. Please check permissions and make sure the object is not in development mode: and (Subject LIKE %something%))) ORDER BY Subject ASC ^ ERROR at Row:4:Column:18 line 4:18 no viable alternative at character '%'. Original queryString was: '.........'

1. The only solution to this type of error is to revise the filters. We have seen that the "greater than" or "lesser than" filters are usually to blame. For example if you say that a field is greater than "blank" it will break. This one is easy to fix, as you can change it to say that the field is not "blank" for the same effect, and this will not break the code.

CHAPTER 2

ADVANCED CONFIGURATION

(PAID VERSION ONLY)

In this chapter you will learn how to quickly configure List Browse for usage in Lightning after paying for the upgrade

---

Several basic steps must be completed in order to install and configure List Browse in your Salesforce.com org. Any user with administrative skills should be able to install and configure the app.

The main steps necessary to complete are listed below.

Step

Description

1 Install and Configure List Browse as shown in chapter 2.

2 Go to www.ListBrowseApp.com and pay for the upgrade. If you have more than 10 users who need List Browse, please contact sales@toafinish.com for a discounted quote.

3 Add the Browse button to any of the 6 standard objects which come with the app

4 Create custom Lightning pages or modify existing custom ones to add the List Browse lightning component.

5 Leave **List Browse** a 5-Star Review on the AppExchange!

Note: Before going on, you must first install the List Browse app as shown in the previous chapter.

PURCHASING THE UPGRADE

How many users will need List Browse? If ten (10) or less users, go to ListBrowseApp.com and pay for the upgrade. In the notes for the order, please include the Org ID of your Salesforce org, in case we cannot match you based on your email address.

If you have more than 10 users who need List Browse, please contact sales@toafinish.com for a quote rather than purchasing the licenses directly.

Once you have purchased the upgrade, allow 4 hours (usually much less) for your org to be upgraded. Once it is upgraded, you will be sent an email letting you know. You can proceed with the next steps at that time.

Note: The "My Domain" feature in Salesforce must be enabled and deployed to users before you can use the Paid version. The reason is that it includes a Lightning Component, and My Domain is necessary for Lightning Components.

LIST BROWSE CONFIGURATION PAGE

To configure how List Browse works, you will want to go to the List Browse Configuration page by going to Setup Installed Applications List Browse Configure. Or, you can also click the apps icon on the top-left of the page and search for "Configure" to go to the Configure page directly, or "List Browse" to go to the App.

Once on the page, there are a few things you can configure:

1. Enable **List Memory** in order to "remember" your active Browse Lists from day to day. Without this, you may have to start over each day.
2. Enable **List Pervasiveness** in order to always have the List Browse component visible on the page, whether the current record is being browsed or not. Without this checked, if the "X" button is pressed, the List Browse component will disappear until you press the Browse button again.
3. Enable **Back to List** to send the user back to the List view when they press the "X" button on the navigation. Without this checked, pressing the "X" will merely delete the active list and leave the user on the current record.

This page will also instruct the user to add remote sites to the Salesforce org in order to sort the Browse Lists according to what the user sees on the screen. The sites given in the instructions are merely the current org's own URLs, but they are needed in order to use the tooling API to find the sorting of the list. If the given sites are not added to the list of remote sites as described, then all List Browse sessions will sort on the Name field, regardless of how the list was sorted.

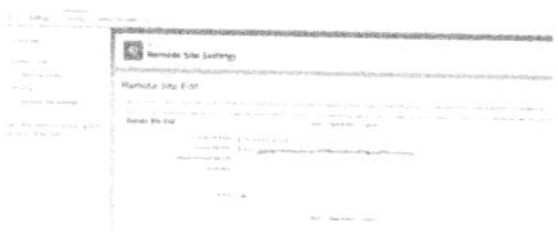

To add the remote sites go to Setup Security Remote Site Settings click the **New** button to add a site. Once you add both sites, refresh the Configuration page and you should see the messages disappear.

ADDING LIST BROWSE TO MORE OBJECTS

Besides the five standard objects that come with the app, you can Browse virtually any other object. To do so, go to Setup Custom Code Visualforce Pages, and press the **New** button to create a Visualforce page that will be used by the "Browse" button. Simply copy the code below into a new Visualforce page, changing the highlighted area with the API name of the object you choose. (When saving, select the option so that it will be available in Lightning):

Custom "Browse Button" Visualforce Page

```
<apex:page
standardController="MyObject__c"
recordSetVar="myrecords"
extensions="taf_listbrowse.PassSelected-
RecordsExt"
showHeader="false"
action="{!createListRecord}">
</apex:page>
```

You can also find the above code in the "pages" folder in our GitHub Repository.

GitHub.com List Browse Sample Code Repository

https://github.com/ToAFinish/listbrowse

Next, you will need to modify the Security of this new page if you want anybody besides a System Administrator to be able to use them. Simply click on the **Security** link next to the page name when looking at your list of Visualforce pages, and select which profiles should have access to it.

Note: if you do not update the Security of your page, your non-Admin users will get an error saying they have insufficient access.

Now, you must add a button for your selected object that uses the "Browse Button" Visualforce page you created above. The options needed are shown below, but the screen will look a little different, depending on the object you selected to add to.

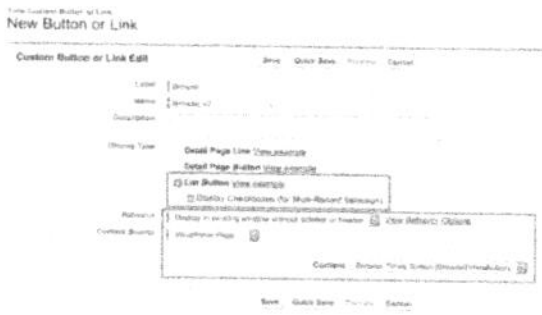

Finally, you need to do the steps referenced in the prior chapter, titled "Configuring the Browse Buttons" to add the button and embed the page for the object you are extending List Browse into. Good luck!

CHAPTER 3

DO IT TO A FINISH

BY O.S. MARDEN

This chapter of the book Pushing to the Front is included for our readers to understand the inspiration which lies behind our work as Salesforce app builders.

YEARS AGO A RELIEF lifeboat at New London sprung a leak, and while being repaired a hammer was found in the bottom that had been left there by the builders thirteen years before. From the constant motion of the boat the hammer had worn through the planking, clear down to the plating.

Not long since, it was discovered that a girl had served twenty years for a twenty months' sentence, in a southern prison, because of the mistake of a court clerk who wrote "years" instead of "months" in the record of the prisoner's sentence.

The history of the human race is full of the most horrible tragedies caused by carelessness and the inexcusable blunders of those who never formed the habit of accuracy, of thoroughness, of doing things to a finish.

Multitudes of people have lost an eye, a leg, or an arm, or are otherwise maimed, because dishonest workmen wrought deception into the articles they manufactured, slighted their work, covered up defects and weak places with paint and varnish.

How many have lost their lives because of dishonest work, carelessness, criminal blundering in railroad construction? Think of the tragedies caused by lies packed in car-wheels, locomotives, steamboat boilers, and engines; lies in defective rails, ties, or switches; lies in dishonest labor put into manufactured material by workmen who said it was good enough for the meager wages they got! Because people were not conscientious in their work there were flaws in the steel, which caused the rail or pillar to snap, the locomotive or other machinery to break. The steel shaft broke in mid-ocean, and the lives of a thousand passengers were jeopardized because of somebody's carelessness.

Even before they are completed, buildings often fall and bury the workmen under their ruins, because somebody was careless, dishonest—either employer or employee—and worked lies, deceptions, into the building.

The majority of railroad wrecks, of disasters on land and sea, which cause so much misery and cost so many lives, are the result of carelessness, thoughtlessness, or half-done, botched, blundering work. They are the evil fruit of the low ideals of slovenly, careless, indifferent workers.

Everywhere over this broad earth we see the tragic results of botched work. Wooden legs, armless sleeves, numberless graves, fatherless and motherless homes everywhere speak of somebody's carelessness, somebody's blunders, somebody's habit of inaccuracy. The worst crimes are not punishable by law. Carelessness, slipshodness, lack of thoroughness, are crimes against self, against humanity, that often do more harm than the crimes that make the perpetrator an outcast from society. Where a tiny flaw or the slightest defect may cost a precious life, carelessness is as much a crime as deliberate criminality.

If everybody put his conscience into his work, did it to a complete finish, it would not only reduce the loss of human life, the mangling and maiming of men and women, to a fraction of what it is at present, but it would also give us a higher quality of manhood and womanhood.

Most young people think too much of quantity, and too little of quality in their work. They try to do too much, and do not do it well. They do not realize that the education, the comfort, the satisfaction, the general improvement, and bracing up of the whole man that comes from doing one thing absolutely right, from putting the trade-mark of one's character on it, far outweighs the value that attaches to the doing of a thousand botched or slipshod jobs.

We are so constituted that the quality which we put into our life-work affects everything else in our lives, and tends to bring our whole conduct to the same level. The entire person takes on the characteristics of one's usual way of doing things. The habit of precision and accuracy strengthens the mentality, improves the whole character.

On the contrary, doing things in a loose-jointed, slipshod, careless manner deteriorates the whole mentality, demoralizes the mental processes, and pulls down the whole life.

Every half-done or slovenly job that goes out of your hands leaves its trace of demoralization behind. After slighting your work, after doing a poor job, you are not quite the same man you were before. You are not so likely to try to keep up the standard of your work, not so likely to regard your word as sacred as before.

The mental and moral effect of half doing, or carelessly doing things; its power to drag down, to demoralize, can hardly be estimated because the processes are so gradual, so subtle. No one can respect himself who habitually botches his work, and when self-respect drops, confidence goes with it; and when confidence and self-respect have gone, excellence is impossible.

It is astonishing how completely a slovenly habit will gradually, insidiously fasten itself upon the individual and so change his whole mental attitude as to thwart absolutely his life-purpose, even when he may think he is doing his best to carry it out.

I know a man who was extremely ambitious to do something very distinctive and who had the ability to do it. When he started on his career he was very exact and painstaking. He demanded the best of himself—would not accept his second-best in anything. The thought of slighting his work was painful to him, but his mental processes have so deteriorated, and he has become so demoralized by the habit which, after a while, grew upon him, of accepting his second-best, that he now slights his work without a protest, seemingly without being conscious of it. He is to-day doing quite ordinary things, without apparent mortification or sense of humiliation, and the tragedy of it all is, *he does not know why he has failed*!

One's ambition and ideals need constant watching and cultivation in order to keep up to the standards. Many people are so constituted that their ambition wanes and their ideals drop when they are alone, or with careless, indifferent people. They require the constant assistance, suggestion, prodding, or example of others to keep them up to standard.

How quickly a youth of high ideals, who has been well trained in thoroughness, often deteriorates when he leaves home and goes to work for an employer with inferior ideals and slipshod methods!

The introduction of inferiority into our work is like introducing subtle poison into the system. It paralyzes the normal functions. Inferiority is an infection which, like leaven, affects the entire system. It dulls ideals, palsies the aspiring faculty, stupefies the ambition, and causes deterioration all along the line.

The human mechanism is so constituted that whatever goes wrong in one part affects the whole structure. There is a very intimate relation between the quality of the work and the quality of the character. Did you ever notice the rapid decline in a young man's character when he began to slight his work, to shirk, to slip in rotten hours, rotten service?

If you should ask the inmates of our penitentiaries what had caused their ruin, many of them could trace the first signs of deterioration to shirking, clipping their hours, deceiving their employers—to indifferent, dishonest work.

We were made to be honest. Honesty is our normal expression, and any departure from it demoralizes and taints the whole character. Honesty means integrity in everything. It not only means reliability in your word, but also carefulness, accuracy, honesty in your work. It does not mean that if only you will not lie with your lips you may lie and defraud in the quality of your work. Honesty means wholeness, completeness; it means truth in everything—in deed and in word. Merely not to steal another's money or goods is not all there is to honesty. You must not steal another's time, you must not steal his goods or ruin his property by half finishing or botching your work, by blundering through carelessness or indifference. Your contract with your employer means that you will give him your best, and not your second-best.

"What a fool you are," said one workman to another, "to take so much pains with that job, when you don't get much pay for it. 'Get the most money for the least work,' is my rule, and I get twice as much money as you do."

"That may be," replied the other, "but I shall like myself better, I shall think more of myself, and that is more important to me than money."

You will like yourself better when you have the approval of your conscience. That will be worth more to you than any amount of money you can pocket through fraudulent, skimped, or botched work. Nothing else can give you the glow of satisfaction, the electric thrill and uplift which come from a superbly-done job. Perfect work harmonizes with the very principles of our being, because we were made for perfection. It fits our very natures.

Some one has said: "It is a race between negligence and ignorance as to which can make the more trouble."

Many a young man is being kept down by what probably seems a small thing to him—negligence, lack of accuracy. He never quite finishes anything he undertakes; he can not be depended upon to do anything quite right; his work always needs looking over by some one else. Hundreds of clerks and book-keepers are getting small salaries in poor positions today because they have never learned to do things absolutely right.

A prominent business man says that the carelessness, inaccuracy, and blundering of employees cost Chicago one million dollars a day. The manager of a large house in that city, says that he has to station pickets here and there throughout the establishment in order to neutralize the evils of inaccuracy and the blundering habit. One of John Wanamaker's partners says that unnecessary blunders and mistakes cost that firm twenty-five thousand dollars a year. The dead letter department of the Post Office in Washington received in one year seven million pieces of undelivered mail. Of these more than eighty thousand bore no address whatever. A great many of them were from business houses. Are the clerks who are responsible for this carelessness likely to win promotion?

Many an employee who would be shocked at the thought of telling his employer a lie with his lips is lying every day in the quality of his work, in his dishonest service, in the rotten hours he is slipping into it, in shirking, in his indifference to his employer's interests. It is just as dishonest to express deception in poor work, in shirking, as to express it with the lips, yet I have known office-boys, who could not be induced to tell their employer a direct lie, to steal his time when on an errand, to hide away during working hours to smoke a cigarette or take a nap, not realizing, perhaps, that lies can be acted as well as told and that acting a lie may be even worse than telling one.

The man who botches his work, who lies or cheats in the goods he sells or manufactures, is dishonest with himself as well as with his fellow men, and must pay the price in loss of self-respect, loss of character, of standing in his community.

Yet on every side we see all sorts of things selling for a song because the maker put no character, no thought into them. Articles of clothing that look stylish and attractive when first worn, very quickly get out of shape, and hang and look like old, much-worn garments. Buttons fly off, seams give way at the slightest strain, dropped stitches are everywhere in evidence, and often the entire article goes to pieces before it is worn half a dozen times.

Everywhere we see furniture which looks all right, but which in reality is full of blemishes and weaknesses, covered up with paint and varnish. Glue starts at joints, chairs and bedsteads break down at the slightest provocation, castors come off, handles pull out, many things "go to pieces" altogether, even while practically new.

"Made to sell, not for service," would be a good label for the great mass of manufactured articles in our markets to-day.

It is difficult to find anything that is well and honestly made, that has character, individuality and thoroughness wrought into it. Most things are just thrown together. This slipshod, dishonest manufacturing is so general that concerns which turn out products based upon honesty and truth often win for themselves a world-wide reputation and command the highest prices.

There is no other advertisement like a good reputation. Some of the world's greatest manufacturers have regarded their reputation as their most precious possession, and under no circumstances would they allow their names to be put on an imperfect article. Vast sums of money are often paid for the use of a name, because of its great reputation for integrity and square dealing.

There was a time when the names of Graham and Tampion on timepieces were guarantees of the most exquisite workmanship and of unquestioned integrity. Strangers from any part of the world could send their purchase money and order goods from those manufacturers without a doubt that they would be squarely dealt with.

Tampion and Graham lie in Westminster Abbey because of the accuracy of their work—

because they refused to manufacture and sell lies.

When you finish a thing you ought to be able to say to yourself: "There, I am willing to stand for that piece of work. It is not pretty well done; it is done as well as I can do it; done to a complete finish. I will stand for that. I am willing to be judged by it."

Never be satisfied with "fairly good," "pretty good," "good enough." Accept nothing short of your best. Put such a quality into your work that anyone who comes across anything you have ever done will see character in it, individuality in it, your trade-mark of superiority upon it. Your reputation is at stake in everything you do, and your reputation is your capital. You cannot afford to do a poor job, to let botched work or anything that is inferior go out of your hands. Every bit of your work, no matter how unimportant or trivial it may seem, should bear your trade-mark of excellence; you should regard every task that goes through your hands, every piece of work you touch, as Tampion regarded every watch that went out of his shop. It must be the very best you can do, the best that human skill can produce.

It is just the little difference between the good and the best that makes the difference between the artist and the artisan. It is just the little touches after the average man would quit that make the master's fame.

Regard your work as Stradivarius regarded

his violins, which he "made for eternity," and not one of which was ever known to come to pieces or break. Stradivarius did not need any patent on his violins, for no other violin maker would pay such a price for excellence as he paid; would take such pains to put his stamp of superiority upon his instrument. Every "Stradivarius" now in existence is worth from three to ten thousand dollars, or several times its weight in gold.

Think of the value such a reputation for thoroughness as that of Stradivarius or Tampion, such a passion to give quality to your work, would give you! There is nothing like being enamored of accuracy, being grounded in thoroughness as a life-principle, of always striving for excellence.

No other characteristic makes such a strong impression upon an employer as the habit of painstaking, carefulness, accuracy. He knows that if a youth puts his conscience into his work from principle, not from the standpoint of salary or what he can get for it, but because there is something in him which refuses to accept anything from himself but the best, that he is honest and made of good material.

I have known many instances where advancement hinged upon the little overplus of interest, of painstaking an employee put into his work, on his doing a little better than was expected of him. Employers do not say all they think, but they detect very quickly the earmarks of superiority. They keep their eye on the employee who has the stamp of excellence upon him, who takes pains with his work, who does it to a finish. They know he has a future.

John D. Rockefeller, Jr., says that the "secret of success is to do the common duty uncommonly well." The majority of young people do not see that the steps which lead to the position above them are constructed, little by little, by the faithful performance of the common, humble, every-day duties of the position they are now filling. The thing which you are now doing will unlock or bar the door to promotion.

Many employees are looking for some great thing to happen that will give them an opportunity to show their mettle. "What can there be," they say to themselves, "in this dry routine, in doing these common, ordinary things, to help me along?" But it is the youth who sees a great opportunity hidden in just these simple services, who sees a very uncommon chance in a common situation, a humble position, who gets on in the world. It is doing things a little better than those about you do them; being a little neater, a little quicker, a little more accurate, a little more observant; it is ingenuity in finding new and more progressive ways of doing old things; it is being a little more polite, a little more obliging, a little more tactful, a little more cheerful, optimistic, a little more energetic, helpful, than those about you that attracts the attention of your employer and other employers also.

Many a boy is marked for a higher position by his employer long before he is aware of it himself. It may be months, or it may be a year before the opening comes, but when it does come the one who has appreciated the infinite difference between "good" and "better," between "fairly good" and "excellent," between what others call "good" and the best that can be done, will be likely to get the place.

If there is that in your nature which demands the best and will take nothing less; if you insist on keeping up your standards in everything you do, you will achieve distinction in some line provided you have the persistence and determination to follow your ideal.

But if you are satisfied with the cheap and shoddy, the botched and slovenly, if you are not particular about quality in your work, or in your environment, or in your personal habits, then you must expect to take second place, to fall back to the rear of the procession.

People who have accomplished work worth while have had a very high sense of the way to do things. They have not been content with mediocrity. They have not confined themselves to the beaten tracks; they have never been satisfied to do things just as others do them, but always a little better. They always pushed things that came to their hands a little higher up, a little farther on. It is this little higher up, this little farther on, that counts in the quality of life's work. It is the constant effort to be first-class in everything one attempts that conquers the heights of excellence.

It is said that Daniel Webster made the best chowder in his state on the principle that he would not be second-class in anything. This is a good resolution with which to start out in your career; never to be second-class in anything. No matter what you do, try to do it as well as it can be done. Have nothing to do with the inferior. Do your best in everything; deal with the best; choose the best; live up to your best.

Everywhere we see mediocre or second-class men—perpetual clerks who will never get away from the yardstick; mechanics who will never be anything but bunglers, all sorts of people who will never rise above mediocrity, who will always fill very ordinary positions because they do not take pains, do not put conscience into their work, do not try to be first-class.

Aside from the lack of desire or effort to be first-class, there are other things that help to make second-class men. Dissipation, bad habits, neglect of health, failure to get an education, all make second-class men. A man weakened by dissipation, whose understanding has been dulled, whose growth has been stunted by self-indulgences, is a second-class man, if, indeed, he is not third-class. A man who, through his amusements in his hours of leisure, exhausts his strength and vitality, vitiates his blood, wears his nerves till his limbs tremble like leaves in the wind, is only half a man, and could in no sense be called first-class.

Everybody knows the things that make for second-class characteristics. Boys imitate older boys and smoke cigarettes in order to be "smart." Then they keep on smoking because they have created an appetite as unnatural as it is harmful. Men get drunk for all sorts of reasons; but, whatever the reason, they cannot remain first-class men and drink. Dissipation in other forms is pursued because of pleasure to be derived, but the surest consequence is that of becoming second-class, below the standard of the best men for any purpose.

Every fault you allow to become a habit, to get control over you, helps to make you second-class, and puts you at a disadvantage in the race for honor, position, wealth, and happiness. Carelessness as to health fills the ranks of the inferior. The submerged classes that the economists talk about are those that are below the high-water mark of the best manhood and womanhood. Sometimes they are second-rate or third-rate people because those who are responsible for their being and their care during their minor years were so before them, but more and more is it becoming one's own fault if, all through life, he remains second-class. Education of some sort, and even a pretty good sort, is possible to practically everyone in our land.

Failure to get the best education available, whether it be in books or in business training, is sure to relegate one to the ranks of the second-class.

There is no excuse for incompetence in this age of opportunity; no excuse for being second-class when it is possible to be first-class, and when first-class is in demand everywhere.

Second-class things are wanted only when first-class can't be had. You wear first-class clothes if you can pay for them, eat first-class butter, first-class meat, and first-class bread, or, if you don't, you wish you could. Second-class men are no more wanted than any other second-class commodity. They are taken and used when the better article is scarce or is too high-priced for the occasion. For work that really amounts to anything, first-class men are wanted. If you make yourself first-class in anything, no matter what your condition or circumstances, no matter what your race or color, you will be in demand. If you are a king in your calling, no matter how humble it may be, nothing can keep you from success.

The world does not demand that you be a physician, a lawyer, a farmer, or a merchant; but it does demand that whatever you do undertake, you will do it right, will do it with all your might and with all the ability you possess. It demands that you be a master in your line.

When Daniel Webster, who had the best brain of his time, was asked to make a speech on some question at the close of a Congressional session, he replied: "I never allow myself to speak on any subject until I have made it my own. I haven't time to do that in this case, hence, I must refuse to speak on the subject."

Dickens would never consent to read before an audience until he had thoroughly prepared his selection.

Balzac, the great French novelist, sometimes worked a week on a single page.

Macready, when playing before scant audiences in country theaters in England, Ireland, and Scotland, always played as if he were before the most brilliant audiences in the great metropolises of the world.

Thoroughness characterizes all successful men. Genius is the art of taking infinite pains. The trouble with many Americans is that they seem to think they can put any sort of poor, slipshod, half-done work into their careers and get first-class products. They do not realize that all great achievement has been characterized by extreme care, infinite painstaking, even to the minutest detail. No youth can ever hope to accomplish much who does not have thoroughness and accuracy indelibly fixed in his life-habit. Slipshodness, inaccuracy, the habit of half doing things, would ruin the career of a youth with a Napoleon's mind.

If we were to examine a list of the men who have left their mark on the world, we should find that, as a rule, it is not composed of those who were brilliant in youth, or who gave great promise at the outset of their careers, but rather of the plodding young men who, if they have not dazzled by their brilliancy, have had the power of a day's work in them, who could stay by a task until it was done, and well done; who have had grit, persistence, common sense, and honesty.

The thorough boys are the boys that are heard from, and usually from posts far higher up than those filled by the boys who were too "smart" to be thorough. One such boy is Elihu Root, now United States Senator. When he was a boy in the grammar school at Clinton, New York, he made up his mind that anything he had to study he would keep at until he mastered it. Although not considered one of the "bright" boys of the school, his teacher soon found that when Elihu professed to know anything he knew it through and through. He was fond of hard problems requiring application and patience. Sometimes the other boys called him a plodder, but Elihu would only smile pleasantly, for he knew what he was about. On winter evenings, while the other boys were out skating, Elihu frequently remained in his room with his arithmetic or algebra. Mr. Root recently said that if his close application to problems in his boyhood did nothing else for him, it made him careful about jumping at conclusions. To every problem there was only one answer, and patience was the price to be paid for it. Carrying the principle of "doing everything to a finish" into the law, he became one of the most noted members of the New York bar, intrusted with vast interests, and then a member of the President's cabinet.

William Ellery Channing, the great New England divine, who in his youth was hardly able to buy the clothes he needed, had a passion for self-improvement. "I wanted to make the most of myself," he says; "I was not satisfied with knowing things superficially and by halves, but tried to get comprehensive views of what I studied."

The quality which, more than any other, has helped to raise the German people to their present commanding position in the world, is their thoroughness. It is giving young Germans a great advantage over both English and American youths. Every employer is looking for thoroughness, and German employees, owing to their preeminence in this respect, the superiority of their training, and the completeness of their preparation for business, are in great demand to-day in England, especially in banks and large mercantile houses.

As a rule, a German who expects to engage in business takes a four years' course in some commercial school, and after graduation serves three years' apprenticeship without pay, to his chosen business.

Thoroughness and reliability, the German's

characteristics, are increasing the power of Germany throughout the civilized world.

Our great lack is want of thoroughness. How seldom you find a young man or woman who is willing to prepare for his life-work! A little education is all they want, a little smattering of books, and then they are ready for business.

"Can't wait," "haven't time to be thorough," is characteristic of our country, and is written on everything—on commerce, on schools, on society, on churches. We can't wait for a high-school, seminary, or college education. The boy can't wait to become a youth, nor the youth to become a man. Young men rush into business with no great reserve of education or drill; of course, they do poor, feverish work, and break down in middle life, while many die of old age in the forties.

Perhaps there is no other country in the world where so much poor work is done as in America. Half-trained medical students perform bungling operations, and butcher their patients, because they are not willing to take time for thorough preparation. Half-trained lawyers stumble through their cases, and make their clients pay for experience which the law school should have given. Half-trained clergymen bungle away in the pulpit, and disgust their intelligent and cultured parishioners. Many an American youth is willing to stumble through life half prepared for his work, and then blame society because he is a failure.

A young man, armed with letters of introduction from prominent men, one day presented himself before Chief Engineer Parsons, of the Rapid Transit Commission of New York as a candidate for a position. "What can you do? Have you any specialty?" asked Mr. Parsons. "I can do almost anything," answered the young man. "Well," remarked the Chief Engineer, rising to end the interview, "I have no use for anyone who can 'almost' do anything. I prefer someone who can actually do one thing thoroughly."

There is a great crowd of human beings just outside the door of proficiency. They can half do a great many things, but can't do any one thing well, to a finish. They have acquisitions which remain permanently unavailable because they were not carried quite to the point of skill; they stopped just short of efficiency. How many people almost know a language or two, which they can neither write nor speak; a science or two, whose elements they have not fully mastered; an art or two, which they can not practise with satisfaction or profit!

The Patent Office at Washington contains hundreds,—yes, thousands,—of inventions which are useless simply because they are not quite practical, because the men who started them lacked the staying quality, the education, or the ability necessary to carry them to the point of practicability.

The world is full of half-finished work,—failures which require only a little more persistence, a little finer mechanical training, a little better education, to make them useful to civilization. Think what a loss it would be if such men as Edison and Bell had not come to the front and carried to a successful termination the half-finished work of others!

Make it a life-rule to give your best to whatever passes through your hands. Stamp it with your manhood. Let superiority be your trademark, let it characterize everything you touch. This is what every employer is looking for. It indicates the best kind of brain; it is the best substitute for genius; it is better capital than cash; it is a better promoter than friends, or "pulls" with the influential.

A successful manufacturer says: "If you make a good pin, you will earn more money than if you make a bad steam engine." "If a man can write a better book, preach a better sermon, or make a better mousetrap than his neighbor," says Emerson, "though he build his house in the woods, the world will make a path to his door."

Never allow yourself to dwell too much upon what you are getting for your work. You have something of infinitely greater importance, greater value, at stake. Your honor, your whole career, your future success, will be affected by the way you do your work, by the conscience or lack of it which you put into your job. Character, manhood and womanhood are at stake, compared with which salary is nothing.

Everything you do is a part of your career. If any work that goes out of your hands is skimped, shirked, bungled, or botched, your character will suffer. If your work is badly done; if it goes to pieces; if there is shoddy or sham in it; if there is dishonesty in it, there is shoddy, sham, dishonesty in your character. We are all of a piece. We cannot have an honest character, a complete, untarnished career, when we are constantly slipping rotten hours, defective material and slipshod service into our work.

The man who has dealt in shams and inferiority, who has botched his work all his life, must be conscious that he has not been a real man; he can not help feeling that his career has been a botched one.

To spend a life buying and selling lies, dealing in cheap, shoddy shams, or botching one's work, is demoralizing to every element of nobility.

Beecher said he was never again quite the same man after reading Ruskin. You are never again quite the same man after doing a poor job, after botching your work. You cannot be just to yourself and unjust to the man you are working for in the quality of your work, for, if you slight your work, you not only strike a fatal blow at your efficiency, but also smirch your character. If you would be a full man, a complete man, a just man, you must be honest to the core in the quality of your work.

No one can be really happy who does not believe in his own honesty. We are so constituted that every departure from the right, from principle, causes loss of self-respect, and makes us unhappy.

Every time we obey the inward law of doing right we hear an inward approval, the amen of the soul, and every time we disobey it, a protest or condemnation.

There is everything in holding a high ideal of your work, for whatever model the mind holds, the life copies. Whatever your vocation, let quality be your life-slogan.

A famous artist said he would never allow himself to look at an inferior drawing or painting, to do anything that was low or demoralizing, lest familiarity with it should taint his own ideal and thus be communicated to his brush.

Many excuse poor, slipshod work on the plea of lack of time. But in the ordinary situations of life there is plenty of time to do everything as it ought to be done.

There is an indescribable superiority added to the character and fiber of the man who always and everywhere puts quality into his work. There is a sense of wholeness, of satisfaction, of happiness, in his life which is never felt by the man who does not do his level best every time. He is not haunted by the ghosts or tail ends of half-finished tasks, of skipped problems; is not kept awake by a troubled conscience.

When we are trying with all our might to do our level best, our whole nature improves. Everything looks down when we are going down hill. Aspiration lifts the life; groveling lowers it.

Don't think you will never hear from a half-finished job, a neglected or botched piece of work. It will never die. It will bob up farther along in your career at the most unexpected moments, in the most embarrassing situations. It will be sure to mortify you when you least expect it. Like Banquo's ghost, it will arise at the most unexpected moments to mar your happiness. A single broken thread in a web of cloth is traced back to the girl who neglected her work in the factory, and the amount of damage is deducted from her wages.

Thousands of people are held back all their lives and obliged to accept inferior positions because they cannot entirely overcome the handicap of slipshod habits formed early in life, habits of inaccuracy, of slovenliness, of skipping difficult problems in school, of slurring their work, shirking, or half doing it. "Oh, that's good enough, what's the use of being so awfully particular?" has been the beginning of a life-long handicap in many a career.

I was much impressed by this motto, which I saw recently in a great establishment,

"WHERE ONLY THE BEST IS GOOD ENOUGH." What a life-motto this would be! How it would revolutionize civilization if everyone were to adopt it and use it; to resolve that, whatever they did only the best they could do would be good enough, would satisfy them!

Adopt this motto as yours. Hang it up in your bedroom, in your office or place of business, put it into your pocket-book, weave it into the texture of everything you do, and your life-work will be what every one's should be—A MASTERPIECE.

AFTERWORD

FEEDBACK AND SUPPORT ACCESS

Please send us your feedback to support@toafinish.com, and don't hesitate to email if you have questions about these instructions. When you do, you might want to give us remote access, as shown in the screenshot below, so that we can log in as you to see the problem.

RATING LIST BROWSE

We greatly enjoy being able to provide users with and app they will find useful. So, if you like the app, please leave us a positive review on the AppExchange:

https://appexchange.salesforce.com/listingDetail?listingId=a0N3000000B3fiZEAR

But if you run into issues, *please* don't leave them there for the world to see (unless we can't get it resolved). Rather, contact us at support@toafinish.com and we'll work together to make this app To A Finish™.

Thank you!

The To A Finish™ team.

Made in the USA
Monee, IL
04 November 2026

67384562R00036